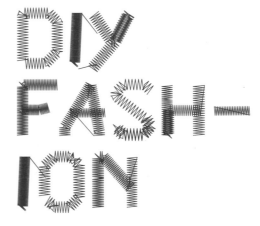

DIY FASH- ION

Laurence King Publishing Ltd
361–373 City Road
London EC1V 1LR
Tel: +44 20 7841 6900
Fax: +44 20 7841 6910
e-mail: enquiries@laurenceking.com
www.laurenceking.com

A catalogue record for this book is available
from the British Library

ISBN: 978 1 85669 653 1

Illustrations: Laura Tinald
Design: TwoSheds Design
Senior editor: Peter Jones

Printed in China

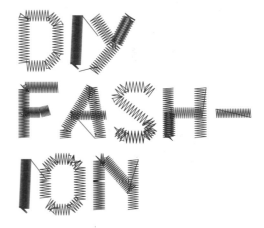

DIY FASH-ION

Contents

6 Preface

Introduction

8 How To Think Outside the Box
10 Your Clothes, Your Inspiration
12 Fashion, Ecology and Value For Money
13 Recycling - Did You Know?
14 Fashion vs Style
17 Fabrics
18 Colour
20 Places to Shop For Ideas
22 Cut-out-and-keep Board

1 Top Secrets

27 Reshaping
28 Slashing Techniques
30 Adding Texture and Colour
32 How To Make a Boob Tube
34 Ribbons and Buttons
36 The Cashmere Cardigan
38 Relief Techniques

2 We Love Hand-me-downs

42 Did You Know?
44 Grandma's Cardigan
46 Ten-minute Make-over
48 Boyfriend's Jumper
50 Dad's Unwanted T-shirt
   Part One - The Skirt
   Part Two - The Dress

3 Denim

56 Did You Know?
58 The Denim Dress
62 The Short Denim Skirt
64 The Long Denim Skirt
66 Shorter Skirts and Bags
68 Cushions and Throws
70 Denim Ties
72 Denim Ideas

Elegance On a Shoestring

4

78 Style At a Steal
80 Elegant Lace Dress
82 Shirt Skirt and Dress
85 The Memory Shirt
86 Halter-neck Scarf Top
88 Antimacassar Halter-neck Top
90 Tea-stained Dress
92 Military Wear

Jewellery, Bags and Accessories

5

98 Brooches, Bracelets and Beautiful Bags
100 The Musical Clutch Bag
102 The Little Suede Evening Bag
104 The Ever-evolving Free Magazine Bag
106 The Lace and Pearls Shopper
108 The Felt Floral Shopper
110 Animal-print Design Evening Bag
112 Classical Evening Bag
114 CD Necklace
118 The Cassette Tape Necklace
120 Other Necklaces
122 Jam Jar Bracelet
124 Floral Brooch
126 Ties From Trimmings
128 The Pop Art Hat

Fittings and Fixings

6

132 Need To Know
135 If the Shoe Fits
136 Be Prepared
138 How To Cheat
140 What To Do With a Hole

144 Credits

Preface

Ever since I was a child I have found it hard to throw things away. I suppose that hoarding is a part of who I am. "It may come in handy one day" is a philosophy that I have always lived by.

As an adult, nothing has changed. Every corner, cupboard and drawer is filled to the brim with bits of fabric, buttons, old shoes, old fashion postcards and any other object d'art that I may deem a precious commodity. This may seem a little over the top to most people, but there is a modicum of method in my madness.

My father always taught me "Waste not want not," and my mother said, "Always wear clean, matching underwear in case you get hit by a bus". Somewhere along the way was born my desire to look good without breaking the bank, my desire to customize.

Decluttering is great for your soul, but sometimes recycling old items can be far more satisfying; it is more gratifying than retail therapy – and it costs little or nothing.

Before You Start Any Projects

For some projects I have, for dramatic effect, used quite bright-coloured fabrics and threads to give a striking look. But these are just guidelines, and as you are the designer and these are your designs, it is up to you to add, take away or change any part that you desire.

Have fun, this book is not a bible, enjoy it and celebrate your successes and achievements. Always remember this phrase if you make a mistake: "Serendipity. It is meant to look like that!"

How To Think Outside the Box

"Every artist was first an amateur"
– Ralph Waldo Emerson

With every new skill comes an education. Everybody has the ability to be creative in one way or another, whether we think what they produce is in good taste or not. It is the skill to unlock your creativity that is the art.

When starting a new idea, it is very easy to dismiss things as "rubbish" but it is all about developing that "rubbish" into something that you can be proud of. Thinking outside of the box is a good place to start. It's all about the apparently ludicrous becoming real.

Example 1: I want a cool newspaper T-shirt

Blue-sky idea:

– A top made from newspaper is not practical.

First moderated idea:

– A top with newspaper stuck on is better, but not practical.

Second moderated idea:

– A top with a newspaper print on – how?

– What technique could I use to put a newspaper print onto a top?

– Research and experiment.

You can tone your idea up or down as many times as you like, until you get it to the point where you like it. Using this course of action may sound like a laborious task, but it will soon become second nature.

Another way of approaching the task is to be completely methodical, keeping a selection of existing ideas in reserve and applying them in turn to the garment in question – this would suit those of a more logical mind.

Example 2: I want a sparkling vest for Saturday night

– Flick through magazines, books and fashion websites to find a top that you like. Look at pp.20–21 for some extra ideas.

– Find a plain top of a similar shape. (Hopefully you can find one in your wardrobe. If not, rummage through the charity shops.)

– Find a technique that suits your design-paint, glitter, or even your jewellery.

– Play around with the idea until you like it, and then make it.

Remember...

Borrowing ideas is not copying. Fashion styles recur so much that it is getting harder to tell what is real vintage and what is not. But creating is being creative. So don't worry that you may be copying the ideas that have inspired you. All the best designers do it.

Your Clothes, Your Inspiration

Wearing nice clothes is all about feeling good. We wear specific clothes to display a part of our personality that we want to share with others. A fun top can show that you are playful and up for a laugh. A smart blouse means that you want to be taken seriously.

We use our clothes like a tribal tattoo. It can denote the music that we like or the 'scene' that we are into. It can also represent the class we wish to be perceived as.

But there is nothing nicer than going out and people commenting on how lovely you look, especially if you do not know them. Take note of these times, for they are the ones when not only have you got it right but you also appear comfortable with your look. There is no point wearing something that you love but that just does not feel good. It can spoil the night. Friends are rarely honest when you look awful in something. So, if someone does say "that colour really suits you" or "that top is so flattering on you" take it on board.

Play with styles and shapes until you feel satisfied you have a look that suits. Remember that most of us do not look like the models in magazines or mannequins, and, by developing your own style and formulating a series of colours and designs that suit you, you can look great at any time.

Almost everyone can wear black or white, so if you are not sure what suits you, try a few styles in simple tones.

Fashion, Ecology and Value For Money

While environmental issues and recycling are at the forefront of our minds, there is also a trend that contradicts all our recycling efforts. Low-cost, mass-produced clothing and accessories are flooding the retail market. Not only are they less cost-effective than you think, they are also environmentally unsound.

If you calculate the amount of wear that you get out of a good-quality piece of clothing, and then compare it to the item that you bought cheaply for a holiday — that you only wore once because you washed it and it lost its shape — the more expensive item would be far greater value for money.

While it seems like a good idea to have a wardrobe bursting with clothing that you may have only worn once and will probably never wear again, what is the point? As irrational, self-conscious females, we are still going to say that we have nothing to wear.

House clothes — you know, the ones that you keep for DIY or cleaning — should be kept to a minimum. Capsule wardrobes are a fantasy to most of us and rather impractical for day to day living, but the more clothes that you have strewn around your bedroom, the more difficult it is to decide what to wear.

What should you do with unwanted clothing? There are several choices, which once you have made them, will help you sort clothing out into four piles:

– Items that you want to keep
– Expensive items that you do not want
– Items that are decent but could use a revamp
– Items that need to go to the recycling bank.

If you have any sentimental clothes that you want to keep, such as a wedding dress, put them in an old suitcase or bag that is moth-proof and store them away under the bed or in the loft. Sell anything that is worth something (it would be very silly to customize designer clothes and handbags that may be worth a buck or two). If it is too shabby to customize, take it to a clothing recycling bank. Even rags can be recycled.

Don't forget to take off any sexy buttons or trims, fringes and ribbons that you may be able to use for future projects.

Polyester, the most widely used manufactured fibre, is made from petroleum.

Recycling – Did You Know?

China has emerged as the largest exporter for fast fashion, accounting for 30% of world apparel exports.

Early humans also recycled their materials. Animal parts that could not be eaten were used to make weaponry, clothing and tools. Those cavemen were much more resourceful than we thought!

90%
of old clothing can be recycled

40%
can be worn again

15%
(wool and acrylics) can be used in the 'shoddy' trade to make new garments

15%
can be 'flocked' and used as mattress padding

20%
can be used as wiper cloths to clean with.

According to The New York Times, spending on clothing and footwear in 2007 was:

$429.8 billion in the US

$87.7 billion in the UK

$85.7 billion in Germany

$28.2 billion in India

$3.8 billion in Kazakhstan.

The first textile recycling started about 200 years ago in the Yorkshire Dales. The rag-and-bone men collected clothing, handbags, bedding and old curtains to sell abroad.

80% of clothing donated to charity shops is sold to textile companies.

Fashion vs Style

It's too, too easy to buy this month's fashion magazine, flick through the pages and rush down to your local high street to 'get that look'. No, no, no, no, no!

Before you fall into that trap of sheep shopping and leg it to your nearest clothing chain, take a closer look and ask yourself a few simple questions:

- Is the colour right for me?
- Is the shape right for me?
- Do I have the arms or legs to carry off that look?
- Is it worth the money? (£35 for a cotton T-shirt is madness)
- Will it last the test of time? Can I still wear it in 8–12 months?

- Do I really need it? Probably not, but, will I regret not buying it? There is no such thing as fashion essentials, only fashion indulgences.

Fashion is exactly that. It's fickle, here today gone tomorrow; attitude is fleeting and not particularly fussy about whom it excludes. If you have a large bust, large arms, tummy or hips, then big patterns are to be avoided like the plague. Very few people look good in leggings and thank heaven that the second time around they have been teamed up with longer, more flattering tops that are more discreet for ladies with bulges and muffin tops. Hot pants and mini skirts are great for girls without curves, but don't kid yourself that if it's 'in vogue', it is a winner.

Fabrics

If possible, try to stick to more natural fabrics. Wool, cashmere, tweed, leather, denim, cotton, silk and linen are timeless, but be aware of colours and shapes as these are the key elements that make it fashion or style. Stick to a simple, classic shape that can be accessorized. Shiny fabrics with stretch are not classy. They will not last, they catch on things and snag and cannot be repaired seamlessly when damaged.

It is harder to simplify a fussy outfit than jazz up a boring one. The little black dress is the perfect example. It is an eternal style that girls of all generations, size and shape can look fabulous in. Wide-bottomed trousers in a good, heavy fabric can also look good on anyone if worn in the correct way (tall ladies in flats and shorter ladies with heels). The legendary styles of the '20s and the '50s are my personal favourites — iconic film stars in beautiful clothes. The tailored cuts of cloth from these two decades still do not look out of place in any stylish joint. In contrast, the fashions of the '60s through to the '90s still seem to be too much 'of the time', reflecting the new technologies of the computer and the new man-made fabrics that became available during this period.

Denims are all about what you feel comfortable in. I have yet to walk into a shop and find the 'perfect' pair for me (after two children, I have big hips in comparison to my waist), but I've found that charity shops are a good place to start as they have jeans from all eras, and of all shapes and sizes, and they are about an eighth of the price. The big bonus of buying second-hand jeans is that they already have a real, gritty, worn-in look — something that denim manufacturers copy these days, but don't always get quite right.

Colour

Seasonal colours can be tricky, and, as with shapes and patterns, can only be worn by some. Yellow is the prime example. It is loud and can be unkind. Some colours may bring out your eyes and others may make you look pale or unhealthy. No matter what your colouring, there will always be a shade that will drag you down and another that will enhance your best features.

Different groups of people believe in different ways to tell what tone or colours you should wear – whether it be to do with seasons or where the stars were when they were born. I think the easiest way to find out is to hold a piece of fabric (not too small) up to your face, just under the chin, and see for yourself. You can usually tell if a colour or tone heightens or detracts from your own tones and features. Never believe that blue is the new green. Green is green and, if it does nothing for you, move on. Remember tone and colour are not the same thing. Try different tones of the same colour and do not rule a colour out just because you tried it once.

Style will always favour black and white, navy, cream, dark grey; gold and silver are great for evenings; and red for flamboyance. Experiment until you find the colours that are right for you.

Places To Shop For Ideas

No matter where you are in the world, there will be inspiration in abundance.

Design is everywhere. Religious buildings are often a veritable feast of patterns and beautiful craftsmanship. Old and new buildings can be used to generate new ideas. Take a look at sculpture both inside and outside buildings, and wood carvings and art that are used to decorate these structures. Look at the way that colours are put together, whether they match or are contrasting.

Window Shopping

Browsing the designer shops is a great way to stimulate the creative juices, borrowing ideas and being influenced by their work. Vintage clothing shops give you a sense of past fashions and styles, and are great for clothing reinvention.

Every country you visit will have a market, each one featuring fantastic cultural designs to be inspired by. Even from city to city cultural identity will vary. Absorb these themes and patterns by picking anything that catches your eye; store your ideas using a notebook, camera or sketch pad.

Pick up free catalogues from anywhere and everywhere to help you brainstorm. Simple bathroom wallpapers could influence a top, an outfit or a whole wardrobe.

Museums and Galleries

Both historical and modern art can suggest techniques and styles of design. You may find inspiration in an installation, in a sculpture or a painted image that you relate to. Museums and galleries also give you an insight into the clothing of the past, and shapes and styles that suit your idea of beauty.

Libraries

A library is a great place to find everything you want under one roof, and it is free. Remember that it is not just the fashion section that will provide advice, tips or guidance. Take a look at the following areas:

Photography – within this section you will find fashion photography, which often includes spectacular clothing and settings.

Art from different cultures – Japanese, Indian, Aztec art, and many others, have amazing colours, patterns and designs. This can help with ideas for trims, designs and details. Also have a look at traditional dress from around the world (usually found in the children's department).

Art and fashion through the ages — these can help you understand shapes and styles. Look for books about different crafting techniques such as tie-dyeing, screen-printing and batiking.

Fashion Magazines

See what is going on in the high street or on the couture catwalks, look at what influences the top designers. Use these ideas to keep up to date, but adapt them to your own style. Remember to note down colours, shapes, fabrics, and special features, such as buttons, bows and trims.

The Internet

Browsing the Web is a cheap and easy way to get ideas. Image search engines are a great place to start. You can find iconic images from old movies, from fashion designers, or of celebrities, and all from the comfort of your home. While you are browsing, find out where your local recycling or salvage centre is and how it works. You may be able to collect as well as donate.

Cut-out-and-keep Board

Find a board and hang it on a wall or the back of a door, then pin anything that inspires you to it. This is for when you want to make or redesign a top or outfit and you cannot think of any ideas. Keep it somewhere prominent, so that you see it all the time. The inspiration will be there continuously to guide you towards the look that you want to achieve.

We always get our best ideas and bits of inspiration when we do not need it, so, for those times when you have a mental block, you can refer to your board for ideas.

sterling-silver
gold-plated
jewellery, from
£, by Claire O

a staying power

LIPSTICK
QUEEN

(1) Chinatown Gloss

And the
first time
baby James w
last October. The a
actress, who says she
"one of those people who
doesn't gain weight", showed
she's had no trouble getting
back her super-slim figure.
She looked as radiant as ever
as she threw snowballs
d strutted around in the
signer outfits she's wearing
series six.
s run of Sex And The City
e the last ever, as its

The day may co
a day may come
both SJP and her
Cattrall, who plays ma
Samantha. The pair – who
are best of friends on screen
– are said not to speak once
the cameras stop rolling.

play

PAUL

Sterling
silver and
brown
agate
cuff,
£450, by
Celine

G CU

With a design to suit e
is your ESSENTIA

Swarovski crystal and
metal cuff, £625, by Rosso
& Brooks

Metal and snakeskin cuff, £180,
by Kara Ross at Browns

SHOP FOR THE HOTTEST NEW
ACCESSORIES AT ELLFUR.COM

jenny8

If you think that's
funny, wait till you
see the back of
her coat

Who else could
manage heels on
those cobbles?

Most designers start with a blank canvas. They have an idea and they develop that idea into a design. When you customize, the designer has already done all the hard work. Your job is to restyle and reinvent. All you have to do is know the key methods of how to do that. Once armed with this information you can adapt it to what suits you.

In this chapter you will learn tricks that will make tops easy prey. The cutting and reshaping makes it feel like a new top, and adding designs of your own makes it feel personal to you.

Remember that all of these projects are just guidelines and can be adapted to suit your needs.

Reshaping

T-shirts can be baggy, shapeless and very unflattering. This is one way of changing your old, unsightly tees and gaining new, funky-shaped tops that you will be delighted to wear.

Step One

Depending on how low you would like the neck of your tee, cut it to where you feel comfortable. It's a good idea to cut it slightly higher than you want it as the fabric will curl back.

Step Two

As with the neck, cut the sleeves to how they suit your body shape and where you feel happy. If you don't like showing off your arms, you can leave the sleeves slightly longer.

Step Three

And the same with the bottom of the T-shirt. You can choose to wear it longer if you're not comfortable showing your derrière. You can also cut the bottom into a bridge shape. The strips left dangling at the bottom can be split and tied to give structure and make your top fitted.

Slashing Techniques

This is a really simple way of adding a little bit of edge to your outfit. And if you are worried that it may make your top too revealing, just pop a little vest underneath. It will still be a top to turn heads.

Hot Tip

It may be a good idea to practise on an old or damaged top first before you apply this to your favourite tee. That way you can hone your slashing technique.

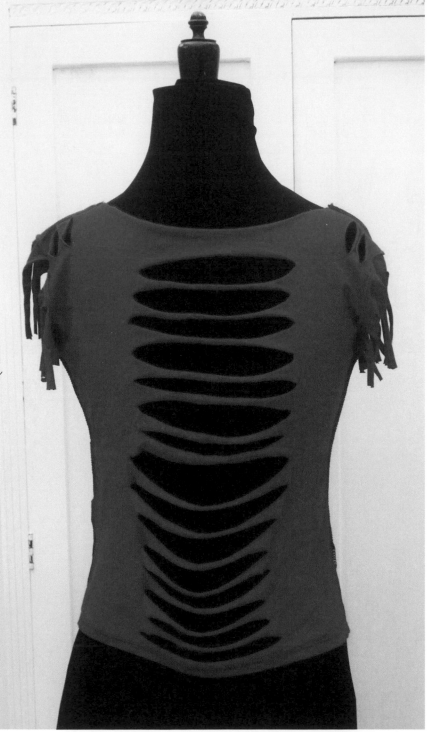

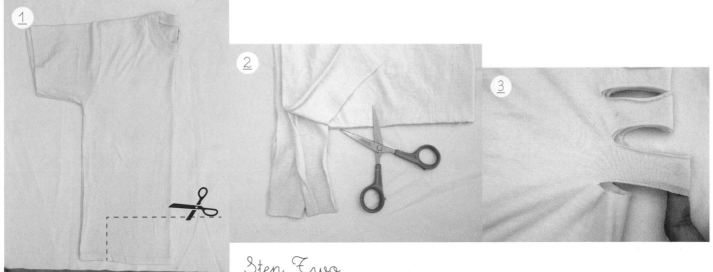

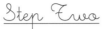

Step One

Fold your T-shirt in half lengthways and cut a rectangular shape out of the middle, leaving the side sections hanging down. You can make the T-shirt as long or as short as you like.

Step Two

Cut the two remaining strips in half, from the bottom of the T-shirt upwards to the point that it is level with the bottom of your T-shirt. Pull the strips taut and let them go. This will make the fabric curl back. You can use these strips to tie up the bottom of the tee.

Step Three

Choose where you want to put your slashes. Cut carefully along the folded edge of your tee. Try to do each slash in one long movement; this prevents you getting jagged edges. Again, pull each strip out to create the curled effect.

Step Four

Follow the same instructions for the sleeves. It is entirely your choice how much or how little you slash your T-shirt. To create the tassled effect shown opposite, cut strips up into the bottom of the sleeves.

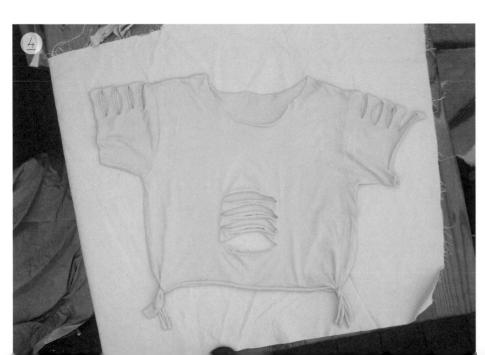

Adding Texture and Colour

Detailing can turn a plain, high-street top into an original piece.

You can use any colour, any fabric, and style it in any way you wish.

Denim scraps, left over from cut-down jeans, are great to use for all sorts of makes. Here is one way to add a personal touch.

Remember

You can also apply this technique to vests or jumpers.

Step One

Follow the reshaping instructions on page 27, cutting your T-shirt to your own specification.

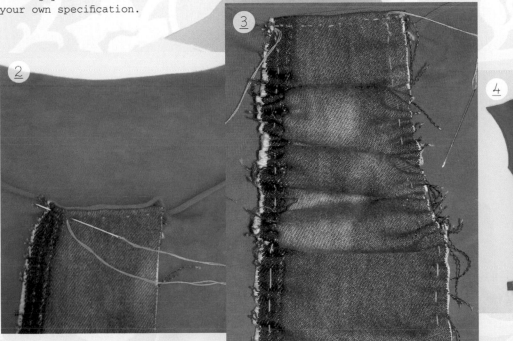
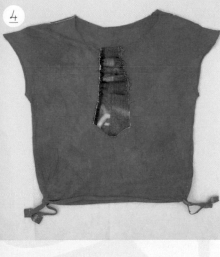

Step Two

You don't have to use denim for this project. Any piece of fabric will work. But do make sure that it has a decent weight to it. Cut it into your tie shape. Fold over the top end of your fabric and sew it onto the neck of the T-shirt.

Step Three

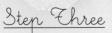

Using a thread of a similar colour to the fabric, sew a running stitch up both sides of your tie. When pulled up, this will make a gathered effect - otherwise known as 'ruches'.

Step Four

When you are happy with the level of your tie, knot the end of the thread on the rear side. If you don't want your tie to swing around when you move about, you could put a small stitch at the bottom to keep it in place.

How To Make a Boob Tube

It's always nice to get a boob tube out in the summer. They are great for holidays, nights out, or just sitting out in the garden. Nobody likes those unsightly suntan strap marks.

Hot Tips

The thicker the fabric, the more support you will get. You can also use a tight T-shirt, but make sure there is enough length in the fabric. If you want your boob tube tighter at the bottom, you could cut slits on either side and tie them together, like in the slashing technique.

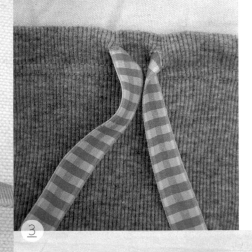

Step One

Find an old or unwanted vest. A man's muscle vest is preferable as it has more length. It needs to have a turned seam at the bottom, but most of them do.

Step Two

Cut it as neatly as possible straight across the front and back under the arm holes. (It may be easier to fold it in half.) The bottom of the vest is now the top of your boob tube.

Step Three

Make a small incision in the centre of the seamed area and attach a small safety pin to a piece of ribbon. Feed the safety pin inside the seam all the way round until it comes back to where you started.

Pull it out through the original hole and tie it in a bow.

That is basically all there is to it!

You can add as many frills and fixings as you desire, or you can keep it simple.

33

Ribbons and Buttons

Sometimes the easiest and simplest designs are the best. This is one of my personal favourites.

Step One

Carefully cut away the neck and a section of the sleeve of your T shirt as on previous projects. Again, take off as much or as little as you want.

Step Two

Select your pieces of ribbon, lace, buttons and anything else that you want to use and place them on your top. Once you have decided on their positioning, sew them into place individually. It's important that you don't group them together to sew them on, because if one comes off, they all come off!

Step Three

You can choose to leave your pieces loose at the bottom or you can stitch them down. But remember that most women are not as flat as a T-shirt, so it may be a good idea to sew the top pieces on first, then try the tee on and pin the pieces in place before you make the decision of where to sew them at the bottom.

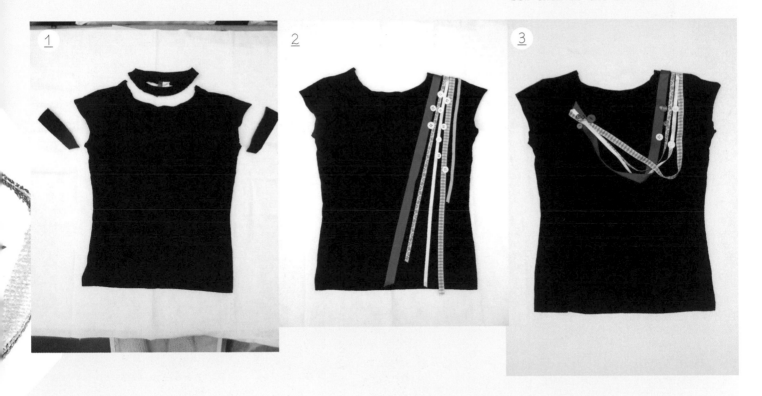

The Cashmere Cardigan

Crop old jumpers and make them into funky, new wraparound cardigans.

Cashmere is great as it does not fray when you cut it.

It's also warm and feels luxurious against the skin.

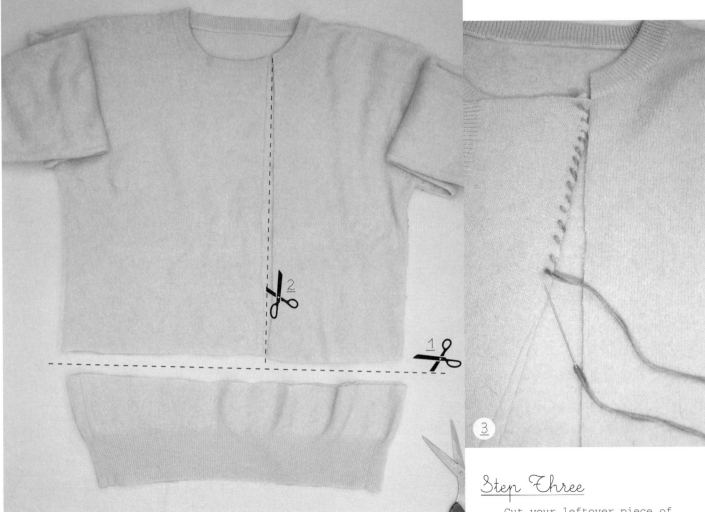

Step One

First, shorten the jumper length. It's up to you how much you take off. You will need a minimum of 6cm (2in) for this make.

It's important that you keep the strip that you remove for the next part of the project.

Step Two

Carefully cut the front of your jumper from top to bottom. You do not have to cut it down the centre. It can look more stylish if you cut it off-centre. It is now starting to take shape.

Step Three

Cut your leftover piece of cashmere in half and blanket stitch each piece to the front of your newly reconstructed cardigan. Make sure that the bottom of the jumper is on the edges of the front to give a nice clean finish.

Embroidery thread is great to use as it comes in great colours and gives a hand-made look. You can add a button, but I find that a kilt pin or a brooch is easier and less time-consuming.

Relief Techniques

This is an easy make that you can use on almost any surface. No skills needed, it is very quick. The more messy you are, the better the effect. Don't forget to protect surrounding surfaces before you start.

Hot Tip

If you are using this technique on painted surfaces, use either a low-tack sticker or put the sticker on a tea towel or piece of fabric beforehand to reduce adhesion.

Step One

Place a piece of card or a few layers of newspaper in between the front and the back of the vest so that the paint does not transfer onto the back of the vest.

Step Two

Lay your stickers in a pattern or in a free-flowing, random way. Once you are happy with their positioning, tape off and cover any areas that you do not want to get paint on.

Step Three

Using a piece of card, plenty of fabric paint and a paintbrush, flick the paint onto the vest. If the paint is runny enough, you can dribble it over or blow it with a straw.

Step Four

Use as many colours as you want. Glittery paints are extremely good for this as they make a sparkle between the colours. Have fun and make a mess.

Step Five

Leave the vest to dry for a couple of hours or overnight. Once it has dried, you can remove the stickers. Remember that all custom-made tops should be hand-washed for a longer life.

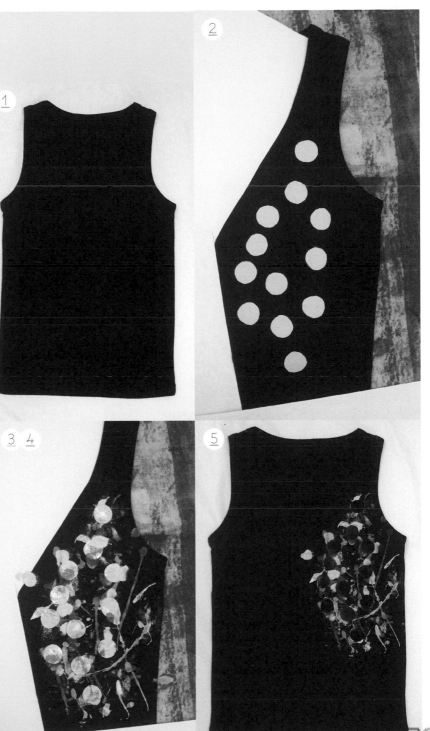

Did You Know?

At different times, throughout the world, rationing has become a part of everyday life. In some parts of the world, it has never been any other way. The recycling of clothing and material has been happening for as long as there have been economic difficulties.

During the 1930's depression in America, women relined their winter coats with old blankets and restyled rags into fashionable items, a huge contrast to the flamboyant attitudes of the roaring twenties.

All over Europe in the 1940's women did all they could to stay glamorous. They would tea-stain their legs to get a healthy, glowing look and because of the lack of stockings they used eyeliner to draw lines up the backs of their legs to mimic the seams. People would also unpick furniture fabrics to make dresses and blouses. They reworked their own clothing and that of their husbands to fit the fashions, one reason why women were more regularly seen in trousers.

Clothing exchanges were introduced where people could swap clothes and shoes with other needy families. These were called 'swap shops' and there were evening classes in local community halls to show people how to make new clothes from old.

Parents have always passed outgrown childrens' clothes around friends and family. When clothing became too small it was passed down to younger children, resulting in the phrase "hand-me-downs". Today good clothing is abundant, but adapting hand-me-downs is still fun to do.

Grandma's Cardigan

Cardigans can be basic and unappealing. Here is just one of many ideas that can jazz up that tired look. By using colours or designs that fit in with other items in your wardrobe, you can also wear it with things that you may not have been able to before.

Step One

Place a piece of card or a few sheets of thick paper inside the cardigan to prevent the paint penetrating to the back.

Step Two

Draw a design of your choice on to a piece of thick paper or card.

If your design is symmetrical, you can fold it to make cutting it out easier. If your design is more complex, you can use a craft knife to make a cleaner edge.

Step Three

Tape your card or paper into place. Choose your colours and, using a big flat-ended brush, dab the paint on. Don't brush it on as this can cause the paint to seep underneath the card.

Step Four

Once the paint has dried, remove the card. Outline your design with black paint or any contrasting colour if you wish. This is not essential but it makes it look neater.

45

Ten-minute Make-over

This is such an easy project that you can do it on a bus, on the train or in front of the telly.

Step One

Find a cardigan, jumper or any other garment you wish to use. Find or buy some bright buttons and some crocheted or lace pieces. Then take a needle and cotton in a contrasting colour.

Step Two

Sit down and decide where to place your bits and pieces and then crack on. If you do not have a great range of coloured buttons, you can paint them with nail varnish. That's it... job done!

Hot Tips

When you visit charity shops or car boot fairs always look at the children's clothes. The buttons are always prettier and, for safety, they have to be of a better quality.

Don't forget to hand-wash hand-made clothes for longer wearability.

Boyfriend's Jumper

Convert your boyfriend's old jumper (or your old boyfriend's jumper) into a funky, sleeveless jumper dress. Just make sure he's finished with it first!

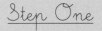

Step One

Remove the neck from the jumper with a sharp pair of scissors. You don't have to worry about fraying as you will be adding to this section.

Remove the sleeves but leave approximately a centimetre (2in) of fabric. Roll the sleeve back twice and stitch it at four points equally spread apart. This will hold the turned-over fabric. Keep the cut-off sleeves as you will need them.

Step Two

Taking the removed sleeves, cut them both open along the seam. Lay one sleeve lengthways with the widest end against the neckline of the jumper. Remember to place your sleeve back to front so that once it is in place it will be the right way around. Put a running stitch all the way across the join between the two pieces and then blanket stitch it. This will strengthen it.

Then do the same with the other sleeve on the back.

Step Three

Sew the two sleeve ends together from the inside. This will function as your new cowl neck. Choose how high you wish it to be.

Cut it and sew it all the way around.

Dad's Unwanted T-shirt

Every man has a T-shirt in his wardrobe that was bought as a holiday souvenir or a present from a relative. Big T-shirts are great for making into loose summerwear. So get those scissors out and start making!

Part One – The Skirt

This skirt is lightweight and will definitely turn heads. You can cut it to any length and by tying up the sides you can use it as beachwear.

Step One

Cut across the top of the T-shirt, front and back, from sleeve to sleeve. The bottom of the T-shirt is now the top of the skirt. Keep the discarded piece as you can use it to make the cord.

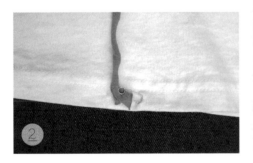

Step Two

Make a small hole through the top layer of the hemmed section (originally the bottom of the T-shirt). Using a safety pin and a ribbon or a length of another T-shirt, feed it all the way round the hem until you come back to where you started. You'll need at least a metre (3ft).

Step Three

Once you have pulled your cord through, take off the safety pin and tie a knot in each end to prevent the thread slipping back in. This make is great because the waist of the skirt is adjustable to fit any size.

Hot Tip

If you want to spice up your skirt, you could cut small slits all the way around the bottom and, using the method in the slashing project on pp.28-29, give your skirt more edge.

51

Dad's Unwanted T-shirt

Part Two – The Dress

The dress is slightly more difficult to make than the skirt, but worth the journey. Once you have made one and you know how to do it, it just gets easier and easier. You can adapt it however you choose and make it your own.

Hot Tip

If you find that you do not have enough fabric for the waistband you can add another piece either from the neck back or from another T-shirt.

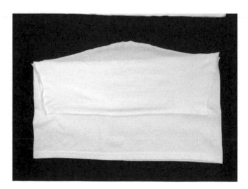

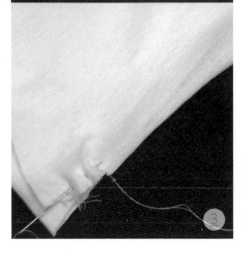

Step One

Using a sharp pair of scissors, cut off the sleeves and the neckband with care. Make sure when taking off the sleeves that you cut after the seam. This helps to keep the structure and prevents the armhole being too large and revealing (unless that is what you want).

Keep the sleeves and collar, you will need them later.

Step Two

Cut your T-shirt in half from one side to the other. If it helps, you can use a pencil or a piece of chalk to faintly mark out your line before cutting.

Step Three

Return to the sleeves that you had previously removed.

Cut them both carefully along the narrow edge (the underarm of the sleeve). Sew these both together lengthways to make a long strip of fabric (left). This will form your waistband.

Step Four

Turn all parts of your T-shirt inside out and sew your sleeve strip to the top and bottom sections, making sure that all the stitching is on the inside. Once you have finished, sew the two end strips together - or if you want, leave the dress open and corset it together with safety pins.

53

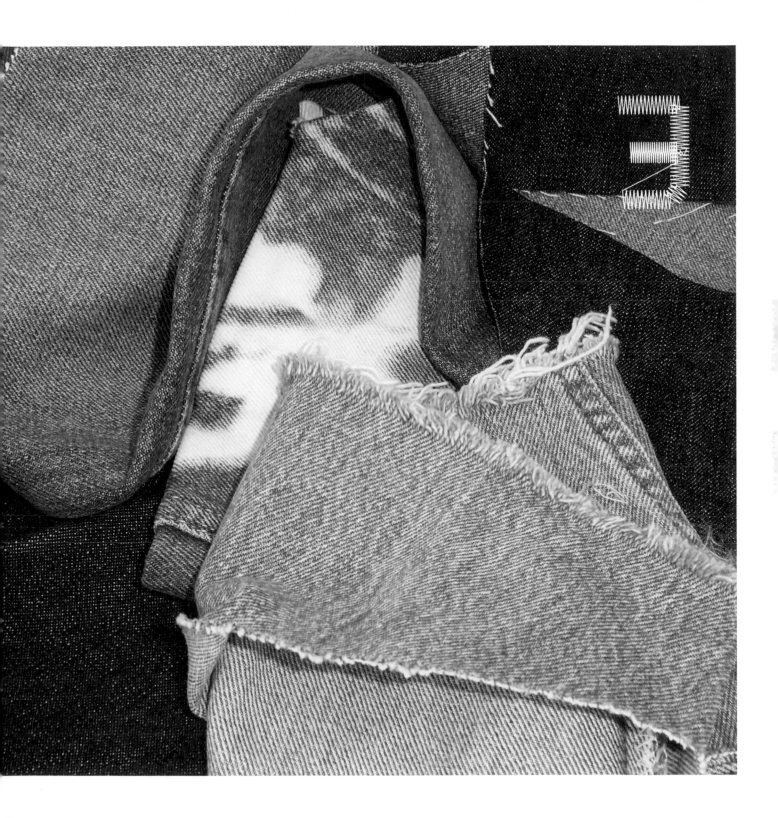

Did You Know?

Denim and jean fabrics have been in use since the sixteenth century. In the south of France a fabric called serge de Nîmes was made and the name was shortened to 'denim'. The name 'jean' is thought to derive from the the name of the Italian city of Genoa where the first denim trousers were made.

Denim is a type of complex cotton fabric. It is woven diagonally for extra strength. It was originally designed for workers in heavy industries.

Levi Strauss & Co. were reportedly the first to make riveted blue 'jeans' out of denim all the way back in 1873. They were made for labourers.

In the 1930's American cowboy films with denim-clad heroes made jeans more mainstream. They were no longer seen as just the labourer's choice of garment.

After the war jeans became leisure wear and in the 1950's Hollywood again pushed denim to the forefront of fashion with iconic stars such as James Dean and Marlon Brando donning tight blue jeans. Denim became the outfit of the '50's rebel.

And the rest, as they say, is history.

The Denim Dress

This is a slightly longer make, but it is one that you can use and re-use for all manner of trousers. The first time is always the hardest but once you know how it is done you will use it again and again.

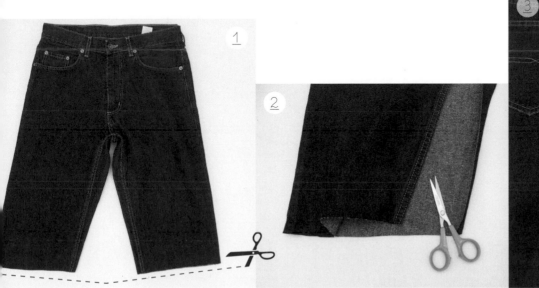

Step One

Offer the jeans waistband up to the top of your bust line and mark where you would like your dress to end. Cut your jeans down to the length that you feel comfortable with. Don't discard your excess pieces of denim. You can use them later.

Step Two

Cut your jeans open, all the way up the inside leg seam. Make sure that you leave the original stitching on the front edge.

If you prefer, you can unpick the stitching. This takes longer and is a lot messier but you do get quite a good effect. If you do choose this option, use a very pointed pair of fabric scissors or a stitch picker.

Step Three

Turn your jeans over and start with the back. Cut along the seam from the crotch up until you reach the level of the bottom of the pockets. Place one side over the other to get a nice flat back and pin it in place. This will reshape the gusset area to stop the back jutting out.

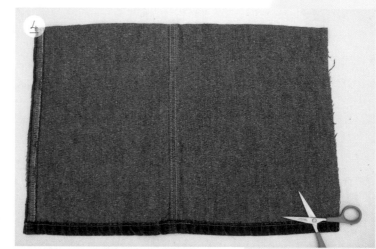

Step Four

Take one of the legs that you removed previously and cut it open on the outside seam. You will need this piece to make up the shortfall of fabric needed for modesty.

5

Step Five

Place your piece of cut-open denim inside the back of the dress opening. Line it up with the bottom edge. Pinch it in the middle and either side of it to create a pleated effect. Pin it in place.

Never sew it straight away. It may move and then will not sit correctly. The pleat will add a small amount of give and design but is not essential. If you prefer it flat, you can do that. I have used the inside of the denim for this section to show the contrast and because I like the edginess. But again, your clothes, your decision.

Hot Tip

You could add a lace underskirt to give that Laura Ashley/Shaker-style look.

Step Six

Turn your dress back over to the front. Cut the front of the jeans from the crotch up to where the zipper or button area starts. Again, place one side over the other and pin flat.

Retrieve the other piece of denim leg that you have left and repeat step four. Insert the denim leg into the front section as before and pin in place. It's up to you whether you wish to pleat the front.

It's a good idea to try the dress on at this point before you sew it to check that you're happy with the fit. But, with all those pins, be very careful!

Once you are pleased with the fit, stitch it and then cut off the excess fabric. Keep the scraps for future projects.

Step Seven

Find an old tie or scarf and knot it through a front belt loop.

Take it over the back and thread it through the belt loop in the middle. Then bring it back over to the other front belt loop to create a dungaree-style shape. Adjust it to where it fits you best and tie it off.

6

7

The Short Denim Skirt

Short denim skirts are great for summer. For travelling, they are effortlessly packed and easy to wear on long journeys.

If you don't feel like baring all, you can layer it by putting them with leggings or tights.

Step One

Offer the jeans up to your waist and mark the length you wish your skirt to be. Then your jeans down to the chosen length.

Step Two

Cut the leg open on the inside leg to create the skirt shape. Don't forget to leave the seam on the front of the skirt.

Step Three

Turn your jeans over and start with the back. Cut along the seam from the crotch up until you are level with the bottom of the pockets. Lay one side over the other to get a nice flat back and pin in place. This will reshape the gusset area to stop the back jutting out.

Do the same on the front, cutting from the crotch up to the zipper or buttons section.

Step Four

Choose a piece of fabric that you think will do your skirt justice. Make sure there's enough to make a matching belt, a minimum of 60cm x 70cm (23 x 28in). Sew it into the triangular area at the front of the skirt.

Depending on how long your skirt is, you may not need a piece in the back. It's up to you.

Step Five

Roll up the remaining fabric and thread it through the belt loops. If it's not long enough, cut it in half lengthways and sew it back together end to end.

The Long Denim Skirt

Old jeans that are ill-fitting or cut unfashionably are good for this make. A long denim skirt is great for summer with a loose top, or in the winter months with boots and tights.

The Easy Option

If you want a quicker alternative, follow steps one to three and wear a long skirt underneath. Then you can transform the look whenever you like by just changing the underlayer!

Step One

Cut the leg open on the inside leg to create the skirt shape. Don't forget to leave the seam on the front of the skirt.

Step Two

Start at the back of the jeans. Cut along the seam from the crotch upwards until you are level with the bottom of the pockets. Place one side over the other to get a nice flat back and pin it in place. This will reshape the gusset area to stop the back jutting out.

Do the same on the front, cutting from the crotch up to the zipper or buttons section.

Step Three

Choose a large piece of fabric big enough to use in the front and the back. I have used a large scarf for this project but you could use denim, an old cotton skirt or even a piece of lace. Pin it into place first and try the skirt on. When you are happy with the look, sew it in to the triangular areas at the front and the back of the skirt. Finally, cut off any excess fabric.

Shorter Skirts and Bags

Short skirts and bags are very similar to make, so I thought that it would be best to place them side by side to save being too repetitive.

The Skirt

Step One

Cut the legs of your jeans off just below the gusset.

Step Two

For the skirt, follow the steps previously used for the short skirt project, but exclude the added fabric. You just have to flat-pin the fabric and sew it.

Step Three

Fray the end using a cheese grater or put it through the washing machine (this also creates a fraying effect). Add any decoration you like.

The Bag

Step One

Follow step one opposite but cut it slightly higher to save having to reshape the gusset area.

Step Two

Turn your jeans inside out and stitch the bottoms of the legs together to form the bag base. Remember that you are going to use it to carry things that may be heavy, so you should try to use a thick, strong cotton and a good pointed needle (a leather needle is good, but very sharp!). Spend a bit of time doing this so that it is well done.

Step Three

Choose a fabric or chain. Here I have used a dog lead that I bought at a car boot fair. Attach it either at the belt loops or sew it in, again using a strong thread.

Cushions and Throws

    With all the leftover legs and scraps that you will have by now, here is a way to use them up. You could save yourself some money by creating great gifts for friends and family.

    Making a throw can be time-consuming, unless you have a sewing machine, but it is a great way to pass the time while watching your favourite soap or listening to the radio.

    All you have to do is, using a strong thread suitable for denim, blanket-stitch your scraps together until you have your desired size or shape. Inside-out pieces add texture and tonal difference, so try to experiment.

    For cushion covers, you can add different fabrics. I backed this cushion in a piece of raw silk for a touch of elegance and luxury. And don't forget to stitch on ribbons or fasteners to prevent the cushion coming out.

    Have fun!

Denim Ties

Denim ties are a great statement for casual nights out. They can be expressive and fun, and can enhance an outfit without effort.

Remember that these ties can be made out of any sturdy fabric.

Step One

Take two scraps of denim. One large piece 40 x 20cm (16 x 8in) and one smaller piece 20 x 20cm (8 x 8in) should be plenty. You will also need a piece of fabric for the back (not shown). A piece 11 x 40cm (5 x 16in) should be sufficient.

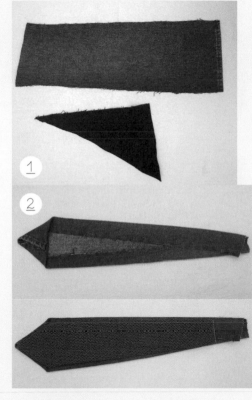

Step Three

Turn your piece back over and place your smaller piece of denim in the shape of a triangle on top. Using a similar colour thread sew this into place. Turn it back over and cross the pieces over. Do this tightly so that it slightly pulls the length of the tie in. Pin this in place, then neatly tuck the remaining fabric into the top.

Step Four

Snip two small holes in the top of the back of the knot and thread a ribbon through. Alternatively, you could sew a brooch clip on. Once you are happy with the way it looks, you can sew it together. If you prefer, you could also use an iron-on glue to put the backing fabric on.

Step Two

Turn your large denim piece over and fold it into a tie shape. Take your piece of fabric and fold this into the same shape but make it slightly smaller, so that the denim edges will extend around the edges. Pin this in place.

Denim Ideas

Style At a Steal

What we wear defines how we hold ourselves. In heels we walk more upright than we do in flats. In tight jeans we walk more seductively than in loose ones. This is maybe due to how we are affected by movies and media. From an early age we absorb the world of beautiful film stars and pop icons. We copy their walks, their style and their dance moves. When we dress up, we imagine ourselves to be those idols. This is what we perceive to be elegance. So when we feel elegant, we hold ourselves elegantly.

Elegance does not have to be the difference between cheap or expensive clothes. It can be achieved through simple tailoring and embellishment. A plain top may not seem elegant but put with a simple string of pearls it becomes an outfit of charm and class. Small touches determine the overall look. This chapter looks at easy ways to make those statements without it costing the earth.

Elegant Lace Dress

This looks a lot more complicated than it actually is. But once you have mastered the technique, you will want to use it over and over.

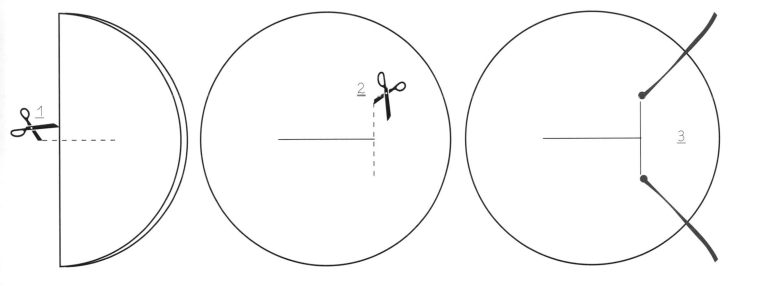

Step One

Fold a round lace tablecloth in half and find the centre. Cut a long opening through the middle approximately 6cm (2½in) longer than half your waist size. This will give you more leeway for adjustment later.

Step Two

Cut the end of one side so that you have a T-shaped slit. Neatly turn back and sew the unfinished edges to give your dress a clean hem.

Step Three

Find or buy a good quality piece of lace, ribbon or fabric and sew two pieces, approximately 60cm (24in) each, to the top of the 'T' shape as illustrated. This will give you the straps for the halter neck. You can then adjust them to fit.

Hot Tip

If you don't like the colour of your lace, you can dye it. Tea staining is easy for a vintage look. See pp.90–91 for the technique. And don't forget to wear something underneath!

Shirt Skirt and Dress

This is a really cool and easy project that should take no more than ten minutes. It's very Vivienne Westwood!

Step One

Men's shirts are usually sold by neck size, which makes it quite easy to work out what size shirts you will need. Two 16-in neck shirts equate to a 32-in waist. It's fine to have it slightly larger, but you never want it too small.

Step Two

Take two shirts. Make sure that they have a similar - or the same - number and settings of buttons. Try to get two that are tonally alike, and have a similar theme or colour. Make sure that your shirts are clean and ironed. Button the two shirts to each other.

Step Three

Take one sleeve from each shirt and loosely tie them together. Do the same on the other side.

For the dress, tie both sleeves around the back. You can add straps if you wish.

Hot Tip

Old military shirts look great in this style and are easy to wear. You could also add some ethnic fabric for a great boho look.

The Memory Shirt

This is my Memory Shirt. When I moved house I found that I had lots of old boxes containing childhood memories – old school patches, Brownie badges and small bits and pieces. So instead of having them hidden away and only seeing them once in a blue moon, I stitched and pinned them to an old army shirt. It hangs at the front of my wardrobe and I can see it all year round.

Halter-neck Scarf Top

This simple summer party top is easy to make and easy to wear. You can make it out of any square of supple fabric (silky materials are best). Obviously, the bigger the piece, the easier it is.

Scarves are easy to come by and are extremely cheap in thrift shops. If you want to be really ostentatious you could hunt out a designer scarf and customize it.

Step One

Find or buy a large, square scarf. Lay it on a flat surface and fold one corner inwards towards the centre. Try to make the fold as even as possible.

Step Two

In a thread of a similar colour to the scarf, sew a hem along the length of the fold, approximately 2cm (1in) from the edge. This will be the hem for your neck strap to go through.

Step Three

Thread an old necklace, a piece of soft ribbon or lace through your hemmed section. Make sure that the piece is long enough to go around your neck and be tied with enough left over.

Step Four

Attach a ribbon to the corners of the scarf either side of the hemmed section. You will use these ribbons to tie the top up around the back. You will need to try the top on and adjust these according to where you wish them to sit – bodies do vary!

Some scarves are long enough to wear as dresses, so why not experiment? You could even sew two together to make a great evening or beach outfit.

Antimacassar Halter-neck Top

Originally used to cover and protect chair and sofa backs and arms, antimacassars are now almost obsolete. They are easy to find in charity shops and at car boot fairs, and you can buy them for a few pennies.

Step One

Cut your antimacassar in half. Lay one of the halves diagonally on top of the other so that they overlap. You will need one other square piece to form the triangle at the front.

Step Two

Sew the halves together in one direction only with a simple running stitch. Once you've reached the end, give the thread a gentle pull to ruche the middle together. Then sew another line of stitches back in the other direction to hold the ruche together.

Step Three

Sew your final piece of fabric into the triangular section in the middle to create a pointed front. If you want a bikini-style top, you can leave this piece out.

Step Four

Sew two ribbons, each about 50cm (20in) long, to the two corners at the top of your design. These will be the straps that tie up around your neck, so make sure that the material you choose is not scratchy against your skin.

Step Five

Sew two more ribbons, about 50-60cm (20-24in) long, to the sides of your newly formed top. These will tie up around the back. As all women are not the same shape, it's a good idea to try the top on and pin the ribbons in place before you commit to sewing them in situ.

Tea-stained Dress

For this project your dress or fabric should be cotton or another natural fabric for the staining to take. The dress shown here started life as an old nightdress.

Step One

Place four tea bags in a half-filled bucket of hot water. Leave them to stew for five to ten minutes. Stir with a wooden spoon, then, wearing a pair of rubber gloves, gently squeeze out as much moisture as possible. Be careful not to split the tea bags.

Step Two

Slowly lower your dress into the water, until it is fully submerged. Don't fold it as this will prevent parts of the dress from absorbing the tea.

Step Three

Using your wooden spoon, stir the fabric. Place a large plate and a cup or other stable, heavy object on top of the fabric to ensure that the whole item is covered in tea. Then leave the whole thing to stand for a few hours.

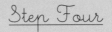

Step Four

Remove the dress from the tea and immediately hang it up to dry. Try to keep the fabric loose while drying. Gathered fabric will cause heavier staining in some areas rather than others and give you an uneven colour.

Once the dress is dry, it can be washed with cold water and worn.

Tea staining can be applied to many items, but nylons and polyester may not take so well, if at all. You can try staining pillow cases, table runners, or just white items that have lost their brightness.

Military Wear

Throughout the second part of the twentieth century military wear drifted in and out of fashion. Ironically, this happened mainly during and after civil unrest in Western countries due to political protest over wars such as Vietnam. It became a uniform for those who were anti-establishment, for people who wanted to represent anarchy (in the punk era), or just wanted to be a little bit different from the rest.

Since the end of the century it has become generic and young people have embraced military wear as their uniform, much like the 'hoodie'.

Military wear can be found in charity shops, flea markets, house clearances and even relatives' wardrobes.

Army surplus stores may be dwindling, but they still exist in certain towns and cities. They may not necessarily sell second-hand or pre-owned uniforms but the internet is abundant with army surplus websites. Many online auction sites also sell military wear.

Army clothing can be redesigned in the same manner that denim can. Because of its function it is very hard-wearing and can last for an age. Thick and robust woven cottons and wools make it easy to re-invent these items. The more tailored garments (for military parades and such) are harder to manipulate because of their rigidity. But this does not mean you cannot have a go.

Here are a few examples of simple makes on lightweight combat wear. By adding lace and trims you can take the edge off the militant look and soften the soldierly effect. Badges and patches work just as well. You can decorate however you feel suits you best. Lightweights are great for painting on as the woven fabric supports the paint in the same way that canvas does.

JEWEL-
LERY,
BAGS AND
ACCES-
SORIES

Brooches, Bracelets and Beautiful Bags

Jewellery can come in an array of guises. Brooches, bracelets and necklaces don't necessarily have to be made of precious metals or jewels. Designers have used every material imaginable to make jewellery — bone and animal teeth, sea and land shells, fruit and seeds, metals and modern plastics, leather and even chocolate. Jewellery is whatever you perceive it to be. On the following pages are a few ideas with an emphasis on waste items. Look around your home and environment to see what other 'throwaway' items can be recycled.

Just as little girls want to be princesses, little bags have a secret need to be beautiful too. A girl can never have enough handbags, they are the epitome of femininity. It's not unusual for women to have two or even three bags running concurrently, depending on the mood of the moment. But sometimes they can get tired-looking, or you can get fed up with them. There are many ways to smarten up a bag and give it a new lease of life. Decoration can be fun or sensible. You can make a political statement with it or change handles, colour and design to reflect your own tastes.

We all see bags that we would love but may think are outside our price range or budget. But who wants a bag that everyone else has anyway? In this chapter are ideas that will help you to make your dreams of a bag, and the bag of your dreams, come true.

The Musical Clutch Bag

'Découpage' (the decoration of surfaces with paper cut-outs) is easy to do and can have a dramatic effect. Whether you use pictures ripped out of magazines, newspapers, comics or (as I have) sheet music, the end result will always be unique.

Hot Tip

You can also change or add a strap to contrast or complement your design!

Step One

Play around with your design and decide how and where you want to place your objects.

Step Two

Prepare the area with PVA glue. Lay your pieces of paper or fabric onto the glue, overlapping each one as you go. Once this is finished, recoat with another layer of glue.

Step Three

After allowing it to dry for a few hours, use paint, nail varnish or permanent marker to outline your design. This helps it to stand out and also gives it a clean, neat edge. You can do this in any colour you like. Glitter paint or varnish is also a fabulous alternative.

Step Four

The final step is to cover the design in a clear varnish. Again, glitter paint or nail varnish can be used. This works as a protective barrier as PVA is water-soluble.

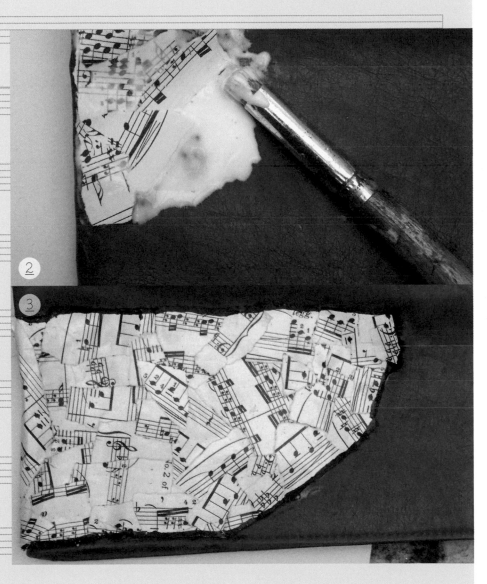

The Little Suede Evening Bag

This make is simple and can be as subtle or loud as you wish it to be.

Hand-painting can be scary for those who are not used to it, but, practice makes perfect! The key is to try your best and to enjoy it.

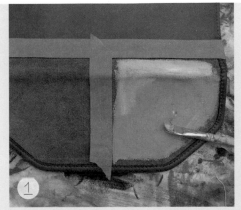

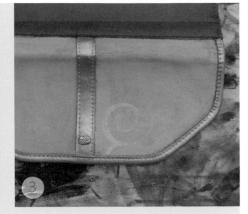

Step One

Mask off the area that you want to paint and brush on a thick layer of colour. Choose a colour that will sit well with the original colour of the bag.

Step Two

After you have allowed the paint to dry, peel off the masking tape and, using a contrasting colour, carefully paint the border and any other parts that you wish.

Step Three

Sketch or practise your pattern or detail, firstly on a scrap of paper or napkin. Once you have chosen your design, paint it onto your bag. Don't be slapdash, it pays to take your time. If you are not confident about your own designs, borrow one from a curtain fabric, wallpaper or textile book. Being inspired is not copying.

Step Four

You can put a layer of varnish or nail varnish over the top for protection, but it is not essential.

The Ever-evolving Free Magazine Bag

At one time or another, we've all been coerced into buying that summer magazine because it has a free sunglasses case, vest or bag. Well, here is something that we can do with those boring old bags to make them a little more cutting edge and personal.

This customization is special because you can change your design as much and as often as you like.

Step One

Take some split pins and gently push them through the fabric and split them. Line the pins up on the inside so that the sides overlap. It's easiest to press down firmly on the pinhead to tighten it into place once the pins are lined up.

Don't use a hammer as this will flatten the domed head.

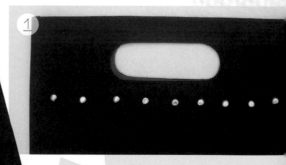

Step Two

Once you've made a row of stud-like split pins, run a piece of sticky tape or fabric tape along the inside over the top of the split edges. This will prevent the pins scraping your hands and arms.

Step Three

On a piece of canvas or any good fabric of your choice sketch your design, first in pencil and then with fabric or acrylic paint. Remember, this is your design!

Because you are not painting straight onto the bag you can play around as much as you like to get the finished piece that you want.

Step Four

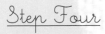

Once you are happy with your artwork, simply safety pin your fabric into place on the front of your bag. This is a great way to express yourself by sandwich-boarding your thoughts or just expressing what's on your mind!

The Lace and Pearls Shopper

With the emphasis these days on not using plastic bags for carrying shopping, this is the ideal make. It's an alternative way to transport weekly wares, it's good for the environment and gives a unique twist and flair to a mundane task.

Step One

Wrap sticky tape around the ends of your pieces of lace to make it easier to thread them though the holes. Weave your lace or fabric in and out of the mesh, making it as even or uneven as you desire. Don't worry if your loops are too long or short, you can adjust them at the end.

Step Two

Thread your pearl necklace into the loops formed by the lace. Push it through the mesh at either end.

Step Three

Further down the bag do exactly the same as in step one but with a contrasting or harmonizing colour or fabric. Add more lace, but this time, just attach it at either end to give a draped feel. If, like me, you only sew when absolutely necessary, you can use a safety pin to secure your fabric from the inside, or alternatively you could use large knots. I have also added an old belt to my bag to give it an ethnic look.

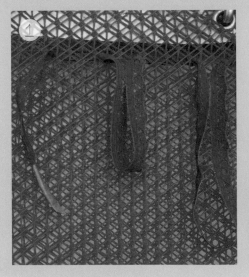

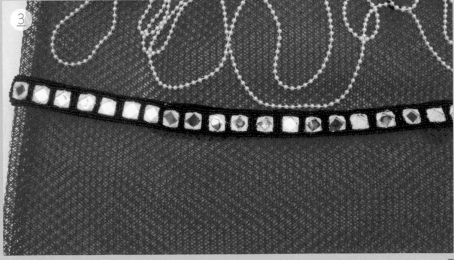

The Felt Floral Shopper

This is a very simple and effective idea. You can use any thick fabric you like.

Felt is fun, inexpensive and easy to use. You can buy it in craft shops or department stores. It is available in great colours and lends a kitsch feel to designs.

Hot Tip

You could also add plastic or fabric faux flowers for a really cool retro effect!

Step One

Cut your felt into any sort of flowers, leaves, insects or anything else that inspires you. Place them in different positions until you feel that you are happy with the result.

Step Two

Where your pieces overlap each other you can either sew or glue them together. This stops the felt flopping forward. Then tack or sew your design onto the bag.

Note that you can't use glue on the bag surface as plastics have a coating which means that the felt will not stick to the bag.

Animal-print Design Evening Bag

If you are not confident about painting directly onto your bag, it may be wise to paint onto canvas or fabric. You can then either sew or glue it onto the bag after it has dried and once you are happy with your artwork.

Easier Option

If you don't feel creative or you just want a quick custom-made look, you could also use a scrap of patterned fabric of your choice and glue or sew this on. Voilà!

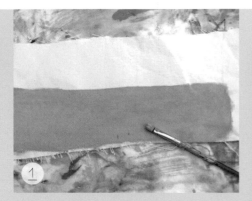

Step One

On canvas, or similar fabric, paint on your base coat. Make sure it is a nice thick layer. It does not have to be yellow.

Step Two

Once the first coat is dry, paint on your secondary colour (the spots). This does not have to be too neat or solid. Use different sizes to get a realistic feel.

Step Three

Add your black detailing around your shapes. Make this outlining solid and don't be shy with your brush. It is integral to the design. Try to paint it unsystematically so that, again, you get a convincing animal-print texture.

Step Four

Glue the finished print to the top of the bag. Add any extras you fancy. On the completed bag (opposite) I have added a tape measure and costume jewellery.

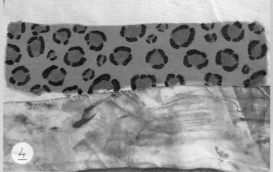

Classical Evening Bag

This quick and easy make is suitable for any sophisticated event and can be customized according to your outfit.

Step One

Collate your chosen pieces for your design. You can get these at charity shops, car boot fairs, sewing shops or grandma's house (do ask permission before you take anything).

Step Two

Play around with your items for a while and once you have decided how you want your completed piece to look, glue or sew them into place.

Obviously, brooches do not have to be sewn on, but if it is not a particularly well-made brooch, it may be a good idea to stick a bit of glue on the back.

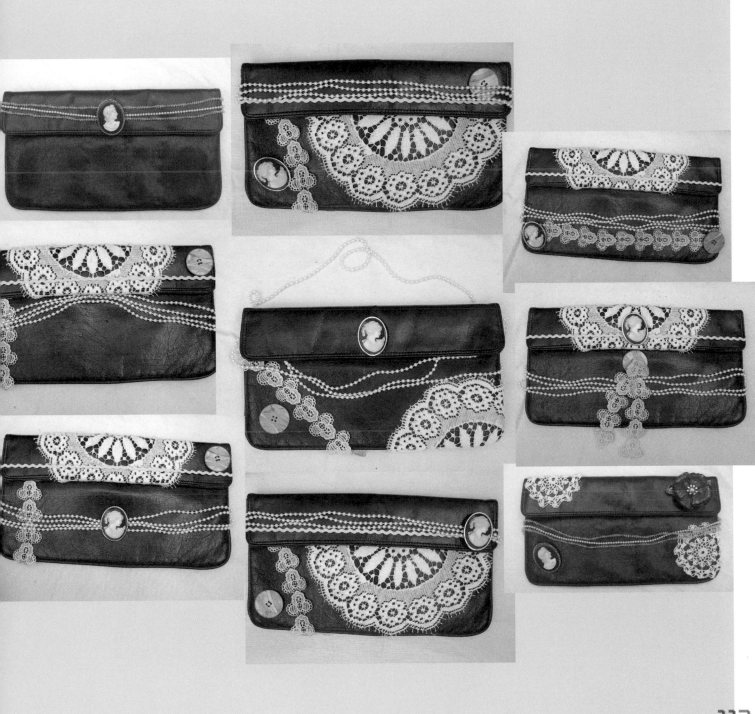

CD Necklace

If you want to stand out in a crowd, this is the piece to wear. Compact discs are everywhere, scratched, damaged or outdated. Here is an idea for how to reuse them and make your outfit shimmer.

Step One

Choose the piece or pieces that you want to use as decoration and position them on your disc.

You can use flat-backed objects, but bonding can sometimes be difficult. Strong glue is advisable. Old clip-on earrings are easy to use as they can be slotted through the central hole.

Step Two

If you choose an element with a back as decoration you may have to pierce the disc.

You can use a small drill bit to make a hole or carefully heat up a pin or wire.

Don't use a nail and hammer as they will crack the plastic.

Step Three

Attach your items and secure the back with double-sided tape or glue; fix felt to the back as a safeguard and to create a clean finish.

If there are any sharp areas on the reverse side, you can pad them before you add the felt or carefully bend them inwards.

Step Four

Secure a ribbon or chain to the back of your disc as your necklace. You can also use it to hold your pierced objects in place.

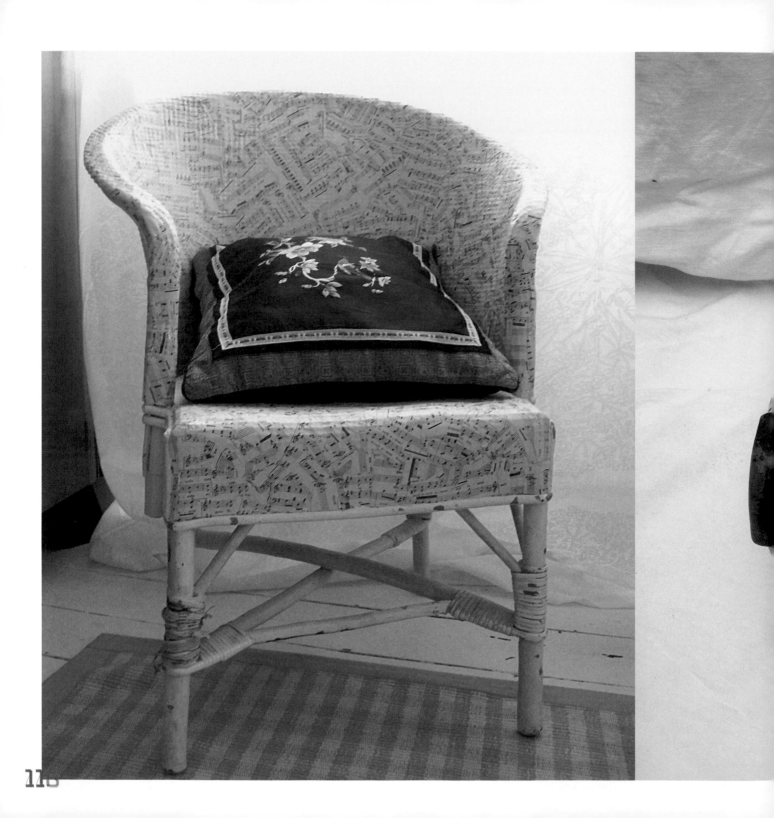

The Cassette Tape Necklace

This is a great way to celebrate the evolution of musical design.

The cassette tape is almost obsolete, but, it's a great iconic form and represents a passing era that will, in years to come, be comparable to that of the gramophone.

You can make this necklace as simple or as wild as you want — or you can leave it just as it is.

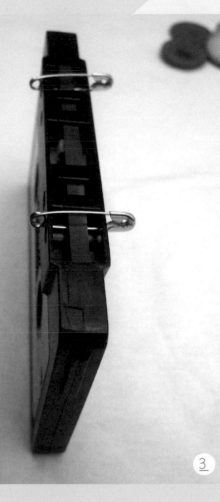

Step One

Decorate your tape using acrylic paint and allow it to dry for a couple of hours.

To speed up the process you can use a hair dryer.

Step Two

For a polished finish, and to protect your painted surface, apply a layer of lacquer or clear nail varnish.

Step Three

On the bottom of the cassette, where the brown tape is, are two sets of parallel holes.

Using safety pins or ribbon, thread your pin or material through either the outer or the inner holes so that they are evenly spaced.

Step Four

Attach your chain or necklace to the safety pins or ribbons.

Other Necklaces

Small toys can be great for making jewellery. Small animals and toy soldiers are perfect for attaching to ribbons or fabric. This can be done using a hot-glue gun or a heavy-duty staple gun. Be careful though, because they are made from hard plastic they can easily crack or break up. Space them evenly for a fun, casual look.

Old cotton reels are easy and quick as they can just be threaded on like beads. Or just use beads.

Jam Jar Bracelet

Jar lids are thrown out daily. We recycle the glass, but the tops seem to just get thrown out with the rubbish. Here is a make that not only uses up your lids but can add a little bit of glamour to an everyday, throwaway item.

Hot Tip

You can stick anything into your bracelet. A photograph or a piece of artwork could be cool. But remember to put a clear, protective layer over the top.

 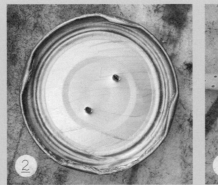 

Step One

Paint your lid front and back and allow it to dry. Once it has dried, you can lacquer it or use clear nail varnish for an extra layer of protection.

Step Two

Using a pointed nail and hammer, carefully make two holes in the centre of the lid about 20mm (³⁄₄in) apart. Make sure that your holes are large enough to thread your ribbon or fabric through. You can use your nail to do this if it is a bit tight.

Step Three

Choose a piece of fabric or felt for your background colour. Place your lid on the fabric and draw around it. Cut it out and glue it into place inside the lid.

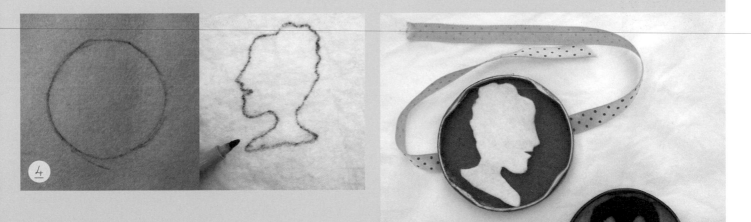

Step Four

Draw your design onto a contrasting piece of fabric and, again, cut out and glue in place.

Floral
Brooch

Scraps of fabric and buttons are things that we all have dotted around. Here is another way of employing these items.

This project takes very little time and the result can be used, not just as a brooch, but as a bag accessory or attached to a ribbon and worn as a bracelet. Have fun, and remember that all the colours and shapes are your choice. These are just guidelines.

Hot Tip
Use bright, contrasting fabrics and buttons to make your flower stand out.

Step One

Choose your floral shape. Draw your shape onto the back of the fabric and cut it out. Use this template to make as many flowers as you wish.

Step Two

Lay the flowers on top of each other in an uneven fashion. This makes the flower look fuller. Sew them together in the centre.

Step Three

Choose a button that suits your fabric colour or colours and sew it into the middle of the flower. At this point, for effect, you can add a leaf or detailing.

Step Four

Turn your flower over and attach a safety pin. Sew this pin on so that it opens outwards. You can then attach the brooch to your jacket or bag.

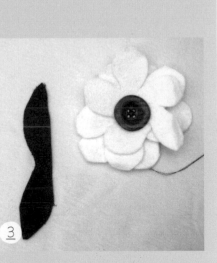

Ties From Trimmings

Trimmings are everywhere. On old dresses, bits of lace, scraps of fabric, ribbons, even bits of old curtains.

This is a really simple way of putting these pieces together to turn something shabby into shabby chic.

There is no exact science or formula for this make. Play around with scraps and decide how you want the piece and how you are going to wear it. It could be a tied necklace, a brooch or a jacket accessory worn on a shoulder or a lapel.

The key is to layer your piece's different items. Place the shorter strands on the top to let the longer pieces hang and peek through from underneath. Choose tones that sit well together and think of the colours that suit you.

Once you have chosen your design idea, sew, pin or tie it all securely together.

Don't forget that you can also use bits of broken jewellery and buttons to embellish your design.

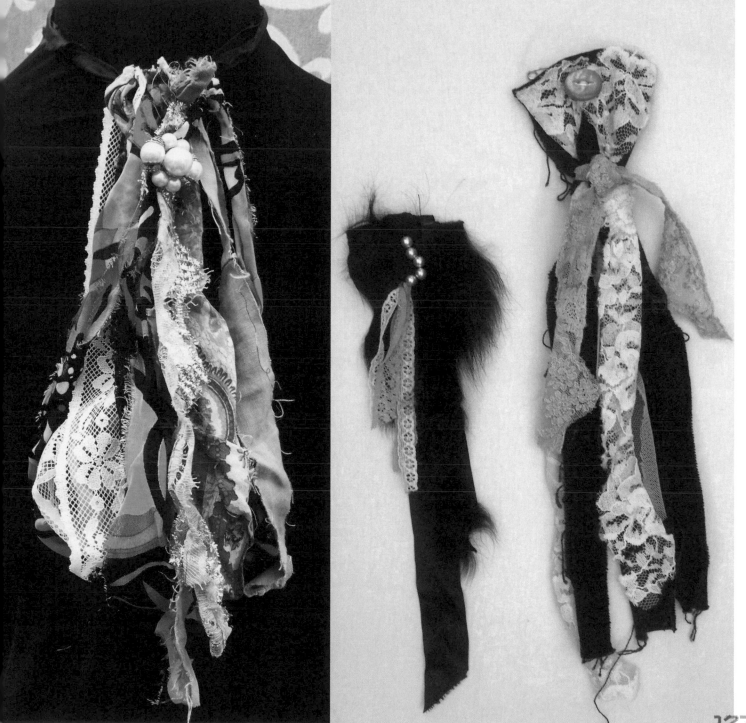

The Pop Art Hat

Hats can be difficult to wear. I like to think of a hat as a true insight into your personality. Some people use hats as a hiding mechanism, some people use them as an extension of their ego, and some people never wear hats at all. Hats are not meant to be modest.

If you wear a hat... make a statement.

Hot Tip
If you have a pretty floral fabric, you could cut out the flowers and stick them on to give an appliquéd look.

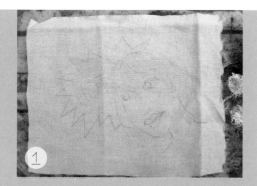

Step One

Faintly draw a pencil sketch of your design onto a piece of cloth. Canvas or a woven fabric such as curtain lining is best. Try not to use too many lines so that they don't show through the paint.

Step Two

Make sure that you have protected the surface underneath your fabric, as paint may seep through. Paint your design in any colour or way that you wish and allow it to dry. For extra impact you can give your design a black outline either in paint or permanent marker pen.

Step Three

Once you are happy with your artwork, carefully cut around your design.

Step Four

There are several ways that you can attach your image. But first you need to decide whether or not to make it temporary or permanent. You can pin it in place using safety pins or big gold studs (or split pins). You could sew it on or you could use an iron-on glue, hot-glue gun or fabric glue.

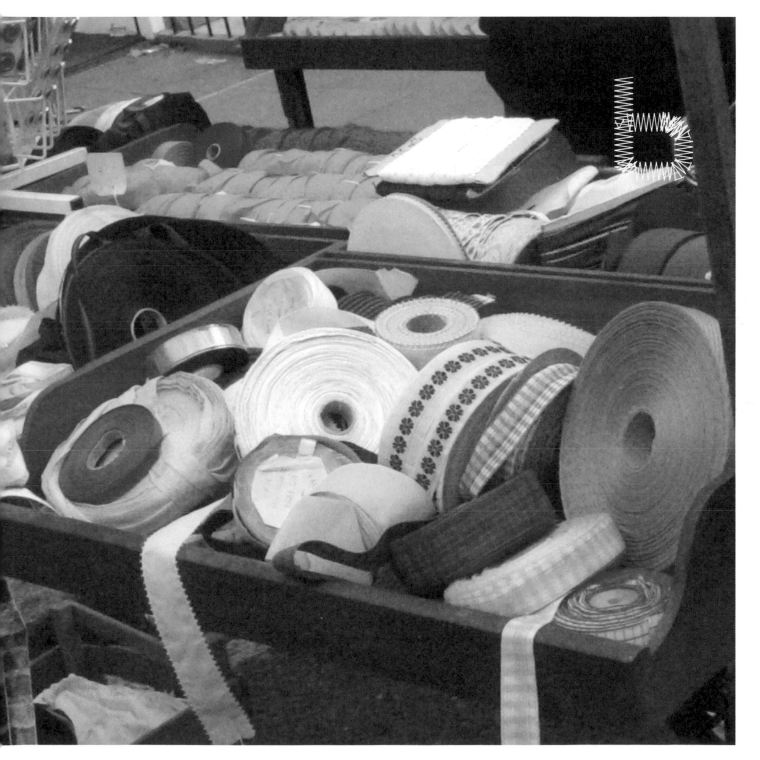

Need To Know

Adam and Eve were said to have worn leaves when they left the Garden of Eden to obscure their natural state. But if silks and pretty fabrics had been available to them, I am sure that Eve would have draped herself in the finest garments. We all have egos, we all want to look our best and we all love something new, but sometimes common sense will tell us that it is simply not justifiable.

New clothes can be expensive, so in the following pages are some pointers on how to save money and reuse what is right in front of you. If there is a hole, it can be fixed. People have done it for centuries. If you can spend a little time on the clothing you have, you can keep your money to spend on those special items that you truly desire.

Adapting or mending clothing not only saves money but gives you a real sense of achievement. It's also a constant learning process.

If the Shoe Fits

Men's shoes can be sexy too. If you are a size six or above, do not forget the men's department. Some men's shoes can look very sexy in small sizes and they are usually a fair bit cheaper. They are also a lot more roomy!

Why not replicate your personal handbag design to put onto your shoes, so that it all matches?

Always buy winter boots in a size larger than you need so that you can wear thick socks or extra layers – they never have your size anyway!

Shoes fit differently in different seasons. If you try on a pair of killer heels in winter, remember that if you have been wearing thick socks and shoes, your feet will be hot and slightly swollen, so you will appear to need a larger size than you do at other times.

Be Prepared

When you are out and about, there are a few things you should carry in your handbag for any clothing crisis or emergency repair.

Wipes and Tissues

If you happen to spill something on your clothing or haphazardly brush against something dirty whilst out, a baby wipe can get it clean.

Firstly, use a tissue to take out as much moisture as possible. Then use the wipe to remove some or all of the remaining mark.

Pins and Ribbons

Safety pins are useful for a missing button or small tear, but can also be a saviour in other situations.

If you arrive at a party with the same dress as someone else, head for the bathroom and, using a few pins, you can adjust your dress by hitching up the sides. You can also pin on a floral hairband or a ribbon to the front to change the look. You could also use a brooch in the same way.

Kilt pins are great for missing buttons on coats or hitching up skirts and dresses. They can also be used on holiday for making large pieces of fabric into sarongs or evening scarves or wraps.

Just like a safety pin, a ribbon can be a life-saver in a crisis. It can be used to close your coat when you have a button missing, to tie your hair back if your hairband snaps, or even to tie up a broken handbag strap.

A Christmas Cracker Sewing Kit

For those who do not mind mending (the old-fashioned way), a small sewing kit can save face, and is the best way of quickly fixing loose buttons or fabric tears.

Take Notes!

And finally, a notepad is a very handy thing to carry. Or if you prefer, a pen and piece of paper. It can be useful if you find yourself in a situation where you want to remember a design idea or a bit of inspiration, especially where photography is prohibited. You can sketch your idea and add notes to help you remember details.

How To Cheat (for the No-sew Brigade)

There are an astounding amount of ways to fake a finish. For the lazy makers (like myself), if you hunt around, you can find so many options that do not include picking up a needle and cotton. If you want to look like you have finished your item properly, you could use some of these tricks.

Certain fabrics can be deliberately frayed to give a purposely unfinished hem. This can only be done with woven fabrics. But do remember that hand-washing is recommended in this case as you do not want your item fraying away to nothing!

Ribbons can be used to lace up the back or sides of a T-shirt instead of sewing it. With thinner fabrics you can tie or knot the fabric so that it fits the way that you want it to.

There are a number of iron-on glues and tapes that you can buy in haberdashery stores to repair tears or holes in fabric. These are easy to use, last quite a while, and give a good, sealed finish.

There is also a huge selection of iron-on materials, and glues that you can use to attach gems to clothing. Look out for iron-on embroidery motifs too.

Make a feature of safety pins. One pin can look like a badly mended repair, but if you use five or six, it starts to look like a design feature. Brooches can be used in the same way.

What To Do With a Hole

Don't be disheartened if you get a hole in a treasured item. It's not for the tip just yet. Here are a few ways to disguise, repair, or make a hole a feature in your much-loved piece.

Sewing up a hole can sometimes look even more unsightly. There are a number of different ways to resolve the problem.

The first is to disguise it. You could use a small motif to cover it (depending on the size of the hole). A pretty fabric can also be used as a patch if sewn neatly; a zigzag machine stitch will give a vintage feel.

If it is a small hole, you can sew on a row of buttons, covering the hole in the process to create a feature out of it.

Leather or denim patches can make items look like designer pieces. But remember to use a suitable needle for either hand or machine work.

Depending on the fabric strength and the type of material, it may be possible to add more holes in a geometric or organic design to incorporate the existing hole. If you enjoy sewing, you could go around each hole with a plain stitch in a contrasting colour to make it look like a designed feature.

Credits

I would like to thank my dear husband Jason and my children Jack and Daisy for putting up with me and supporting me throughout.

Sedley and Rudolph Bryden for encouraging and teaching me, and making me who I am.

Dorota Beau-Ingle and Kate Ferrie for hours of brainstorming, and having faith in my ideas and Dorota's photographic skills

Maurice Nixon and the Portobello stall holders for their help.

I would like to thank the designer Jon Allan, the illustrator Laura Tinald, and Helen Evans, Peter Jones and everyone else at Laurence King for having belief in my dream.